T0023959

A true story from the Bible

JONAH
and the very
BiG FiSH

· WRITTEN BY ·
Tim Thornborough

· ILLUSTRATED BY ·
Jennifer Davison

There are lots and lots of words in the world. And some of them can mean the same thing – or almost the same thing.

This is a book about a very grumpy prophet who learns something very important about God. It uses lots of words that mean the same or similar things.

Perhaps you can think of other words to add?

I hope you like, love, relish and adore reading it!

Jonah and the Very Big Fish © The Good Book Company, 2019. Reprinted 2020, 2021, 2023.
Words by Tim Thornborough. Illustrations by Jennifer Davison. Design and art direction by André Parker
thegoodbook.co.uk • thegoodbook.com • thegoodbook.com.au • thegoodbook.co.nz • thegoodbook.co.in
ISBN: 9781784983796. Printed in Turkey.

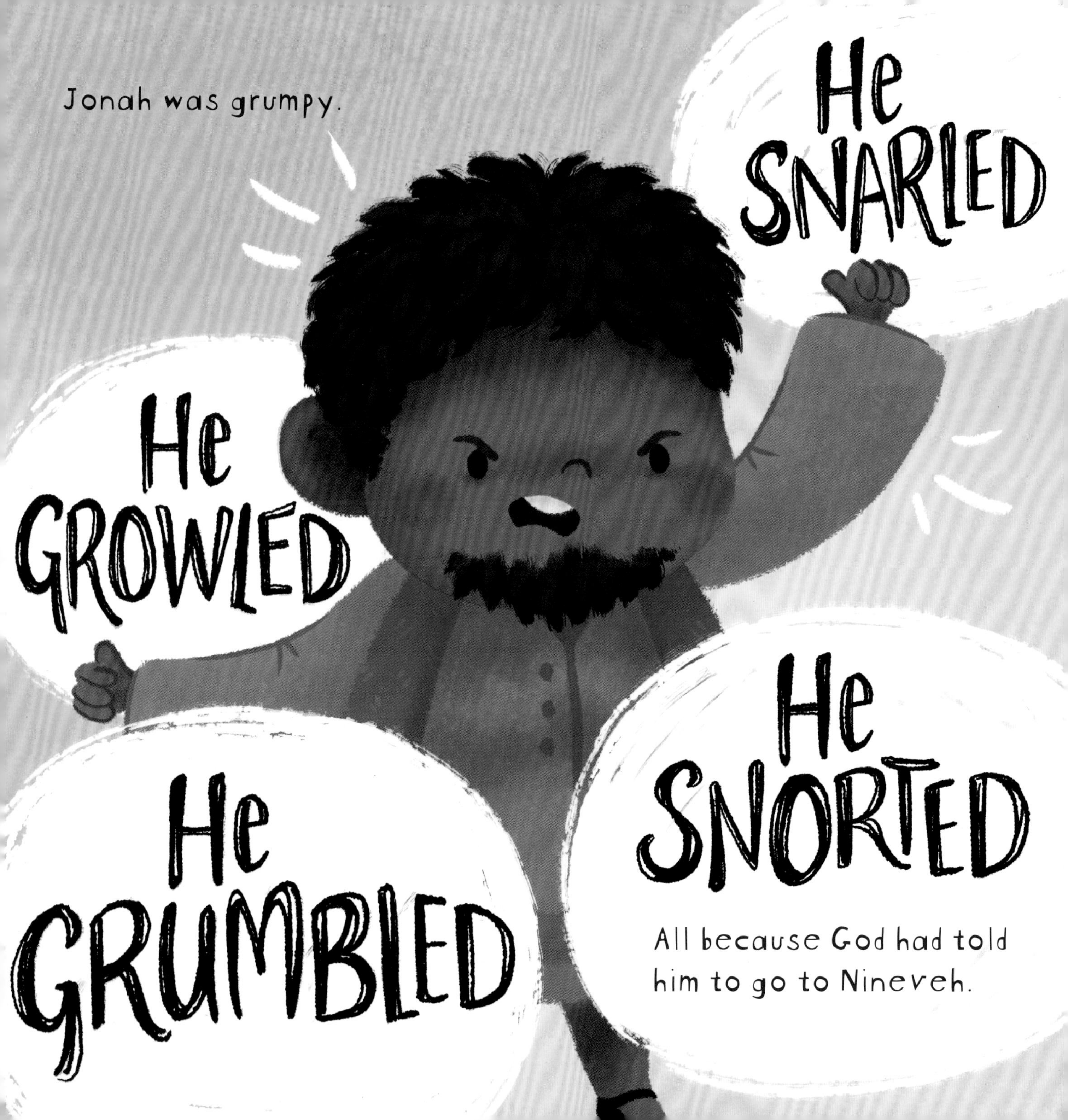

Jonah was grumpy.

He SNARLED

He GROWLED

He GRUMBLED

He SNORTED

All because God had told him to go to Nineveh.

The people of Nineveh were not just bad...

they were NASTY HORRIBLE WICKED CRUEL

They didn't care about other people.

And they didn't care about God.

But God cared about them.

So he told Jonah to go and
give them a message.

But grumpy Jonah didn't want
to go. He said to himself,

"Those people are...

HORRIBLE
TERRIBLE
ABOMINABLE
UNFORGIVABLE

They deserve to be punished!"

So he jumped on a ship and sailed away in the opposite direction.

As Jonah slept, God sent a huge, howling hurricane. The sailors were...

HORRIFIED
TERRIFIED
PETRIFIED
JELLY-FIED

So they woke Jonah up.

"It's all my fault," said grumpy Jonah.
"You'd better throw me into the sea."

The sailors didn't want Jonah
to drown, but they did as they
were told. They hurled Jonah
into the raging sea.

And the sea was suddenly...

CALM
QUIET
STILL
PEACEFUL

The sailors were saved, and they said, "Thank you" to God.

But God had not finished with grumpy Jonah yet...

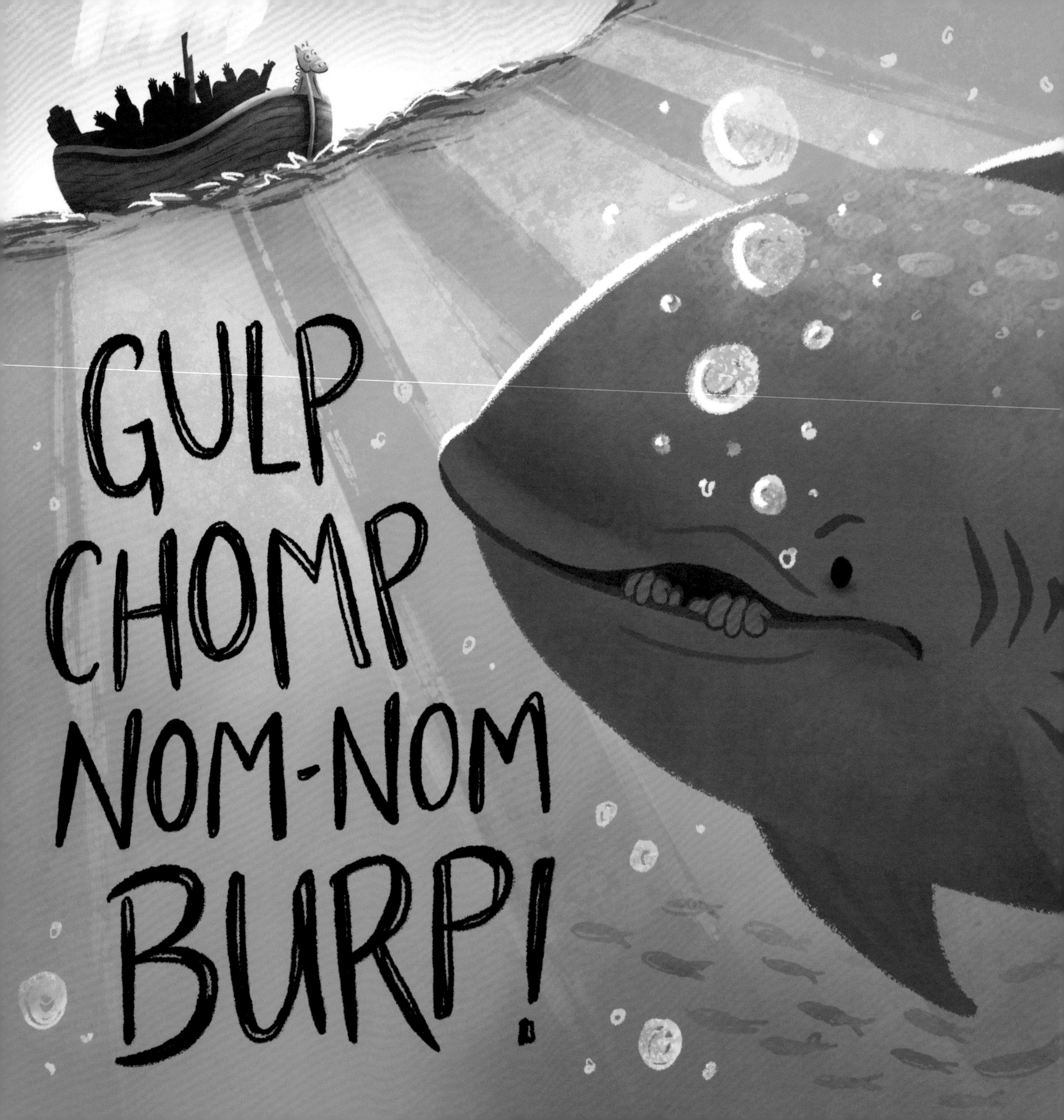
GULP
CHOMP
NOM-NOM
BURP!

God sent a Very Big Fish
that swallowed him whole!

Jonah sat for three whole days
in the belly of the fish.

He realised how wrong he had been. He said, "I've been...

WITLESS BRAINLESS MINDLESS SENSELESS

It's up to God who he saves, not me!"

God heard his prayer and spoke to the fish.

AWK! GAK! HICCUP! BLARP!

And the fish spat him out on dry land.

Jonah went to the great
city of Nineveh and
delivered God's message.

"God has seen how
evil you are. And in
just **40** days you will
be destroyed."

And the people of
Ninevah ...
LISTENED!

They were...

SAD

SORRY

REPENTANT

REGRETFUL

The king and all the people said,
"Let's stop being...

NASTY HORRIBLE WICKED CRUEL

Let's start trying to…

PLEASE GOD

LOVE GOD

PRAY to GOD

and be kind to each other. And let's hope that God has mercy on us."

AND GOD
LOVED THEM
FORGAVE THEM
SHOWED MERCY
TO THEM AND
WELCOMED THEM

But what did Jonah think?
Jonah was angry with God so...

He
GRUMBLED

He
POUTED

He
SULKED

AND HE
GRUMPED

"I knew you would forgive them," he said.

"You are a kind and loving God, and you're always ready to forgive people who turn back to you – however bad they've been!"

God said,
   "You're right Jonah.

I am KIND I am LOVING and I will FORGIVE

ANYONE who turns to me...

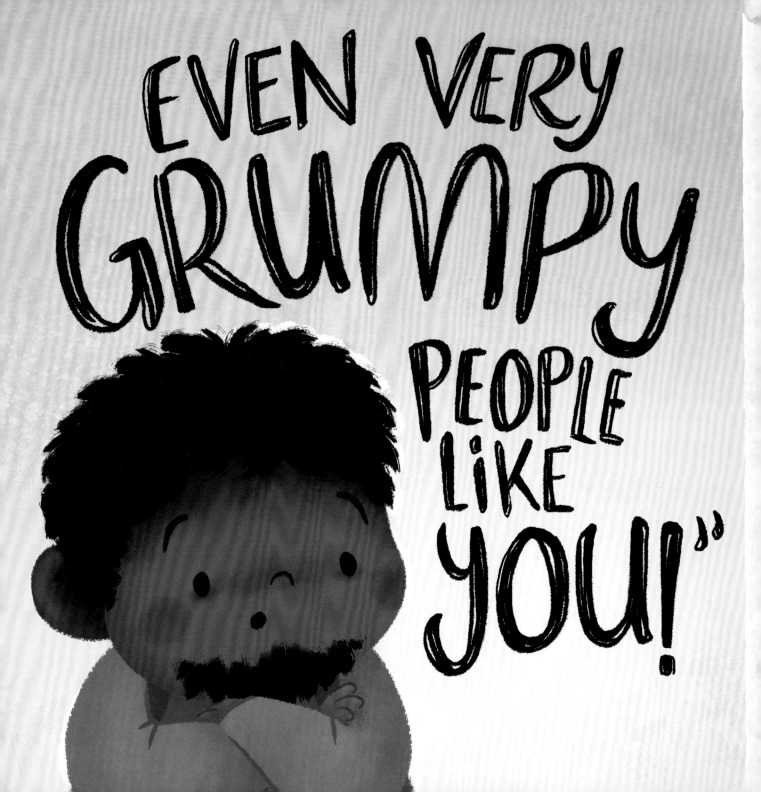